401 design meditations

Wisdom, Insights, and
Intriguing Thoughts from
244 Leading Designers

401 design meditations

Catharine
Fishel

First published in the United States of America by

Rockport Publishers, Inc.
33 Commercial Street
Gloucester, Massachusetts 01930-5089

978.282.9590 Telephone
978.283.2742 Fax

www.rockpub.com

Library of Congress Cataloging-in-Publication Data
Fishel, Catharine M.
  401 design meditations : wisdom, insights, and intriguing thoughts from 244 leading designers / Catharine Fishel.
    p.   cm.
  ISBN 1-59253-127-X (pob)
  1. Design—Quotations, maxims, etc. I. Title: Four hundred and one design meditations. II. Title.
PN6084.D46F57 2005
745.4—dc22   2004025555
                                                         CIP

10 9 8 7 6 5 4 3 2

Cover and layout designed by Timothy Samara

Printed in China

contents

Foreword

I've written books and magazine articles for and about the design field for more than two decades. In all that time, amongst the hundreds and hundreds of designers that I have had the privilege to interview, probably all but a handful have told me that he or she is "not a word person." "I could never do your job," they say.

I've always found this to be a curious protest. Sure, most designers would not aspire to be full-time writers, but the vast majority are, in fact, excellent "word people." Their vocabulary, imagination, empathy, ability to communicate, and tolerance for aggravation all contribute to their prowess. Designers are generally well-read, and they keep up-to-date on cultural matters.

But more than anything else, because so many feel uneasy when forced to actually commit words to print, they are not cavalier when it comes to words. They choose them carefully, and, as a result, they are a delight to listen to.

I was very pleased to have the opportunity to curate this little book for that reason.

Catharine Fishel

Design Is...

1 Design is... a mix of craft, science, storytelling, propaganda, and philosophy.

Erik Adigard, MAD From *Wired* magazine, Issue 9.01, January 2001

2 Graphic design is the spit and polish but not the shoe.

Ellen Lupton Director of the MFA program at the Maryland Institute College of Art

3 Good design is good business.

Thomas Watson, Jr. Founder of IBM

4 Art does not reproduce what we see; rather, it makes us see.

Paul Klee Swiss painter, graphic artist, and art theorist

5 Leafing through an old magazine, I noticed a small ad about a design course by mail. The headline read: "Art for pleasure and profit!" I have never found a better definition to describe my profession. Of course, at times it is more the pleasure and less the profit, at times the contrary. But if one of the components were missing, design wouldn't exist.

Carlo Angelini Principal, Angelini Design

6 Design without thinking is like a story with no plot.

Pat Hansen Pat Hansen Design

7 Design brings content into focus; design makes function visible.

Jennifer Morla Morla Design

8 In our effort to communicate, we strive to present our client's message as clearly and directly as we can. But as designers, there is part of us that is showman, entertainer, artist, and salesman. We cast our line into the vast sea of prospects. Paper, photography, illustration, design, and type act as our bait. If our audience is hungry for a product or service, and if our artistry is effective, we may get a nibble.

Don Weller The Weller Institute for the Cure of Design

9 Clients have no trouble paying $5,800 for an hour in a Gulfstream corporate jet or $425 for a month of parking. But God forbid they spend $3 per on a glossy annual report.

Bill Cahan Cahan & Associates, in a talk to the Association of Registered Graphic Designers of Ontario

good
a (small)

beer

Chinese
tea

sponge cakes —

Singha
Beer

pine apple

C

Jam ro

mangosteam
dark purple

plant
rts

rambutan

green/
orange
red.

mboo
oot

mangostean

curry with
chicken blood
jelly
(didn't try it.)

Sketches by Brian Webb
made in Thailand,
where he had to draw
pictures to ask what
he was eating.

10 What design does is to put us in the driver's seat, or, at
a minimum, to enlist for us the services of an expert driver.
Clement Mok Designer, text excerpted from his website

11 Form follows feeling.
David Turner Principal, Turner Duckworth

12 I would show my jobs to my mother, [and] she would
always say the same thing: "That's nice, dear." And then
she would say, "Did you write it?" or "Did you do the
drawing?" or "Did you take the pictures?" I'd always
answer "no," then I realized the problem. My answer was
then, "I made this happen. It's called design."
Brian Webb Principal, Webb & Webb, formerly Trickett & Webb

13 Design is a response to social change.
George Nelson Architect and industrial designer

14 Design is a better idea.
Steve Sikora Design Guys

Rick Valicenti frequently
uses word play to
connect visual ideas
to spoken ones.

15 I have no ****ing idea
what the future of ****ing design is!
Saul Bass Aspen Design Conference, circa 1983

16 Design should never say, "Look at me." It should always say, "Look at this."
David Craib Parable Design

17 # Form follows dysfunction.
Rick Valicenti Thirst

18 "Graphic:" It means, "Vividly described
in words and images" (and usually refers
to either design or pornography).
David Turner Principal, Turner Duckworth

19 Designers communicate
only three things:
Messages about value,
messages of value,
and messages of no value.
Rick Valicenti Thirst

LIVING

in tense

LIVING

in tents

20 I'm a code breaker. Metaphorically, I combine visual elements like people combine letters or numbers. The right combination is the code for the safe where the solution lies.

Yossi Lemel Principal, Lemel Cohen Design

21 **[Design is] enjoyment with passion.**

Diego Giaccone FutureBrand, Argentina

22 Design isn't about sampling. It is about thinking.

Steve Liska Principal, Liska & Associates

23 Design is not life. Design is a living. But you can design life.

Jack H. Summerford Designer and writer

24 Design is not the private domain of the "best of us" here in the high-and-mighty industrialized world, but the very public human birthright of the "rest of us" in societies the world over. The sooner we understand this, the sooner high design will be acceptable to all.

David Stairs Designers Without Borders

25 Modernism is not a
system of design—
it is a state of mind.

W.A. Dwiggins Book designer

26 Design culture is just another subculture. [Designers are] just like hot rod artists, or psychedelic people, or punks.

Art Chantry Art Chantry Design Co.

27 Good design is a form of respect—on the part of the producer for the person who will eventually spend hard-earned cash on the product, use the product, own the product.

David Brown Former president of Art Center College of Design

28 Design is instilling structure and soul into our naturally chaotic and unintelligible environment.

Laurinda Spear FAIA, principal, Arquitectonica

29 Art is making something out of nothing and selling it.
Frank Zappa Iconoclastic musician, singer, and songwriter

30 Life is the art of drawing without an eraser.
Unknown

31 Great design defies gravity. Try to bury it and it will float back to the top.
Bill Gardner Principal, Gardner Design

32 Many things difficult to design prove easy to performance.
Samuel Johnson English lexicographer

33 Persuading outsiders
to buy and persuading
insiders to believe.

Wally Olins on branding

"Often a rendering will take a turn I didn't expect, as I see something new in the random lines that looks even better than I had hoped, much like looking up at the shifting clouds on a lazy day, and you see an amazing image appear perfectly for a moment. That is the moment you hope to capture in a good sketch," says artist Justin Hampton.

34 But it's so important to remember
that design is a part of life; it is not all of life.

Domenic Lippa Principal, Lippa Pearce Design, from
Inside the Business of Graphic Design

35 **Design can be an elusive mistress. Be good to her,
don't rush things, and she'll probably reward you every time.
Tread lightly, however, as she will ridicule you in front
of your friends and peers if you cross her.**

Justin Hampton Artist and designer

36 Graphic art is my secret garden, the place
where I can get lost but also find territories
I didn't even know existed.

Kari Piippo Graphic designer

37 A life in design is a difficult one—a life living in a state of heightened emotional awareness, throwing your entire soul into your very best work, which may be dismissed in an instant for the most trivial and petty of reasons. I can't think of anything else I would rather do more.

Robert Louey Principal, Louey Rubino Design

38 There are only two types of graphic design: good and bad.

Ken Cato Principal, Cato Purnell Partners

39 Graphic design is a lie... we're lying to ourselves. The reasons young people go into graphic design have little or nothing to do with solving business problems and everything to do with making cool things.

John Bielenberg Principal, C2 LLC

40 Engineering, not science, rules design.

Denise Gonzales Crisp Instructor, from her blog at www.superstove.blogs.com

41 No. It's always been lousy.

Paul Rand Designer, on being asked
if graphic design was any worse than
it had ever been

42 My favorite art definition comes
from Brian Eno, who says to
think of artworks not as objects
but as "triggers for experiences."

Stefan Sagmeister Principal, Sagmeister, Inc.

43 [Design is] the subjective response to objective criteria.

Richard Gluckman Architect

44 [Design is] desire disguised as function.

Terence Riley Chief curator of architecture and design, MoMA

45 Design that moves
others
comes from issues that
move you.

Jennifer Morla Principal, Morla Design

46 Design is the art of situations.

Ellen Lupton Director of the MFA program at the Maryland Institute College of Art

47 Design is the child of the concept "efficiency."

Jorge Frascara From *What is Graphic Design?* published by RotoVision, 2002

48 Design is at base a practical activity, the making of artifacts.

Quenten Newark From *What is Graphic Design?* published by RotoVision, 2002

49 Design needs to extend beyond the artifact.

John Creson Addis

50 Style › "good design" › massmarket › cliché › embarrassment › "it's over" › fetish ›

Lorraine Wild Designer, on the cyclical nature of style

51 Art is about growth.
It's about discovery. The most
important question
is always, "What's next?"

Stefan G. Bucher Principal, 344 Design

52 Design is like life: It is an ongoing process of development and discovery.

Thomas Vasquez Principal, Cyclops

53 Design is a form of justice between men and material.
If this moral tone is offensive to some, remember
that design is concerned with relationships, and relationships
are always good or bad, never neutral.

Alvin Lustig Excerpted from *Nine Pioneers in American Graphic Design,* by R. Roger Remington and Barbara J. Hodik

:vival › interesting › style › "good design" ›…

54 Yes, as a way of determining and influencing people's actions, design is a political act.
Rudy VanderLans Designer; from *Speak Up,* June 2003

55 Design, done well, requires that you be ever-present but invisible.
Greg Galle Designer and member of C2 LLC

56 Bad design is smoke, while good design is a mirror.
Juan-Carlos Fernández Ideogram, Mexico

57 For me, design is like choosing what I'm going to wear for the day— only much more complicated and not really the same at all.
Robynne Raye Principal, Modern Dog Design Co.

58 Designers think, so [people] can feel.
Juan-Carlos Fernández Ideogram, Mexico

True Grit

59 A camel is a horse designed by committee.

Sir Alec Issigonis Automobile designer

60 A common mistake that people make when trying to design something completely foolproof is to underestimate the ingenuity of complete fools.

Douglas Adams Creator of *The Hitchhiker's Guide to the Galaxy*

61 [Our accountant] said it was a terrible idea to go into business with your best friend. So we got a new accountant.

Emily Oberman and Bonnie Siegler Principals, Number 17, from *Inside the Business of Graphic Design*, Allworth Press, 2002

62 I actually dreamt in Pantone.

Clint Runge Archrival

63 Free lemon wafers

Stefan Sagmeister Principal, Sagmeister, Inc., when asked why David Byrne, the Rolling Stones, and Lou Reed came to him to design their CDs

Designer Andrew Lewis,
of Andrew Lewis Design,
calls his Daytimer his
"daydreamer."

64 I was once asked by a client to create a logo that would win an Addy Award. Luckily, I have a drawerful of pencils for just such an occasion.

Rodney Davidson Dogstar

65 What perplexes me most these days is that after hundreds of posters, logos, brochures, and digital bits and pieces, I still start every project gripped by the fingers of fear and failure.

Andrew Lewis Principal, Andrew Lewis Design

66 Naps are completely underestimated and are an essential part of the creative process.

Laura Zeck Short Stories

67 We received an e-mail from a cosmetics company in southeast Asia, asking us to design product packaging. At first, I thought, "Cool. Someone on the other side of the world has contacted us." But ultimately, we didn't respond. The product turned out to be a breast enlargement cream "that really worked."

Jon Wippich Dotzero Design

Wednesday

CALL PAM

HISTLER

GPM
15-5 PM

93-4772

41 DENMANSS

Thursday — Constitution Day 88

ERWIN - Gr
PAUL HAAD - 3862739

EM. CARR - RESUME
DES. 477.4115

FRANK - LODGAWS

Reminders

July   August

FAUSS

---

6 Friday

8 am   CACCS -
○ BUTCHALL
○ VINCOR
ROY & BC MUSEUM
CYNTHIA WRATE

EM. CARR - RESUME VICTORIA WILLS
RETAINE

12 noon
GRANVILLE ISLAND
1 pm   JOE GOETZ

809 - 8030
ERIC

$ 2 - 15%.
1790] 20.
1432]

VANCOUV OPERA - PESSORS

Reminders
LADY
LLANGATTOCK
CONCERTO

September   October
S M T W T F S   S M T W T F S

---

7 Saturday

CUSTOMSTAND
163 CANGFORD
3836171
CLARION - 1315
2" $ 80

11:30 SAUNDERS

8 Sunday

TORONTO → YYZ
9AM →

CREST SIGNS
KELLY 384-
670 BAY

Reminders
VIC WEST
BAM - TYLLEU
WESTCOAST
BROU

68 I have found the best people to work with are gay men. They never want to "run it past their wives."

Rodney Davidson Dogstar

69 "Fuggit." As in, "Two tears in a bucket, (insert word here)," or "Ahhh, (insert word here.)" It's short and not so sweet but it's our shop motto and said at least every day.

Coby Schultz Ames Design

70 Sometimes, when I'm in the middle of a meeting, I want to sit in the client's lap, stroke his hair, and say, "Hey, funny face."

Anonymous From a Potlatch Paper promotion

71 Even when we come up with the perfect solution on the first day, we will still have to spend two more months proving that it is actually the perfect solution.

Scott Mires Principal, Mires Design, from the LogoLounge.com website

72 My wife keeps complaining that I am married to my art. But my art keeps complaining that I am still sleeping with my wife.

Emek Artist and designer

73 "Frankensteining:" The process of collecting graphic parts from different design options and compiling them into one option. You end up with a design solution worthy of a mob carrying torches and pitchforks.

Von R. Glitschka Principal, Glitschka Studios

74 Every night I pray that clients with taste will get money and clients with money will get taste.

Bill Gardner Principal, Gardner Design

75 The client may be king, but he's not the art director.

Von R. Glitschka Principal, Glitschka Studios

76 We have had to face a revolution, the Shah's fall, a new political government, Saddam's invasion, eight years of war, the war's ending, and the beginning of a more open society.

Majid Abbasi Did Graphics, Tehran, on the endurance of Iranian design

77 Curiosity may have killed the cat, but I'll bet she had a really interesting life up until then.

Unknown

78 Never date a girl who works in an art supply store. When the relationship ends, you won't be able to buy supplies anymore.

Rodney Davidson Dogstar

79 When we are angry or depressed in our creativity, we have misplaced our power. We have allowed someone else to determine our worth, and then we are angry at being undervalued.

Julia Margaret Cameron English pioneer photographer

80 We spend
a lot of effort
trying to
make things
look effortless.

Alexander Isley
Principal,
Alexander Isley
Design

81 I am a student—a beginner like you are…
To learn yourself is more difficult than to listen to a teacher.

Alexey Brodovitch Addressing a design laboratory class in 1964, excerpted from *Nine Pioneers in American Graphic Design*, by R. Roger Remington and Barbara J. Hodik

82 Forget about developing a client's imagination.
Give me a client with courage.

Bill Gardner Principal, Gardner Design

From Rastko Ciric's booklet, titled *Vitae Communis Anatomia, which contains 30 anatomical drawings of ordinary objects.*

83 I think about a lineage of painters, who for hundreds of years dragged themselves to their studios each day, with or without patronage, to paint the best damn paintings they knew how to make.

Kim Baer Principal, KBDA

84 The only difference between myself and a madman is that I am not mad.

Salvador Dali Surrealist painter

85 I love the comment, "You must love designing for a living." At that point, I usually start to laugh or break into uncontrollable tears.

Andrew Lewis Principal, Andrew Lewis Design

86 # God save our files!

Rastko Ciric Poster designer and instructor, University of Arts, Belgrade

87 [Design] as a garment is a prickly wool sweater, not warm, cozy velvetine, that we must wear every day.

Andrew Lewis Principal, Andrew Lewis Design

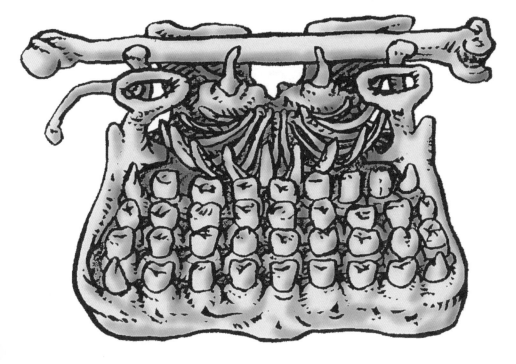

How to put a positive
spin on almost
anything, according
to Von R. Glitschka,
of Glitschka Studios.

88 My first day of working at Rogers-Kellogg-Stillson, a man named Charles Folks
came in with a blank dummy and said, "Here, do *Westvaco Inspirations*."

Bradbury Thompson On a challenge he accepted from 1939 to 1962, excerpted from
Nine Pioneers in American Graphic Design, by R. Roger Remington and Barbara J. Hodik

89 **"Craptacular!" An easy, one-word critique
used to relay your dislike of the work being
presented, while still sounding upbeat.**

Von R. Glitschka Princpal, Glitschka Studios

90 Many musicians have surprisingly unsophisticated visual
vocabularies. Ideas often incorporate big-titted female astronauts.

Stefan Sagmeister Principal, Sagmeister, Inc.

91 A picture is worth a thousand dollars.

Marty Neumeier Neutron LLC

92 Budget determines the vehicle for an idea, not the strength of the idea itself.

Thomas Vasquez Cyclops

93 Making good design is like giving somebody an orgasm: there's a lot of sweat and heavy breathing and sometimes you're totally in the dark. In the end, you just keep fiddling about until you get it right.

Stefan G. Bucher Principal, 344 Design

94 Quality, cost, fast turnaround—choose any two.

Rob Wallace Principal, Wallace Church, Inc.

95 To do what you love to do and do what you hate to do at the same time is to be an artist.

Emek Artist and designer

96 Rejection of our work is something we all have to cope with. Accept "no" as a challenge… Can "no" sometimes be a positive? Yes.

Tony Gable Gable Design Group

97 An understanding wife.

Lester Beall Listing qualifications of a designer in 1963, from an article originally published in the AIGA Rochester newsletter, 1995

98 # Praise be that which makes us hard.

Sean Adams Principal, Adams Morioka

99 My early design work looks like I was sick and my throw-up designed it.

Jesse von Glück Motive Design

100 The kind of effort that goes into graphic expression is essentially lonely and intensive and produces, at its best, a simple logical design. It is sometimes frustrating to find that hardly anyone knows that it is a very complicated job to produce something simple.

William Golden Excerpted from *Nine Pioneers in American Graphic Design*, by R. Roger Remington and Barbara J. Hodik

101 These days all you need is the ability to watch television and hold a potato at the same time to call yourself a designer.

Glenn Martinez Sun Microsystems

102 | **You will never really like anything you do, and you will die knowing that you still have to do your best work.**

Garth Walker Orange Juice Design

103 You can never enter the same river twice, but you can make limited edition [prints] of it.

Emek Artist and designer

104 Never show fools unfinished work.

Michael Schrage Codirector of the MIT Media Lab's e-Market Initiative

105 Design is often and largely a young person's game. It is a jealous mistress and demands so much and gives back so little sometimes. But we sing sweetly to her and defend her virtue regardless. Just when you were tired and fed up and ready to leave, we see her again and return to our divine joy and punishment.

Terry Marks Principal, Terry Marks Design

106 Design's biggest enemy is the high cost of saving money.

Rob Wallace Principal, Wallace Church, Inc.

107 The work is hard, if you can get it.

Steve Sikora Design Guys

108 Never let your clients see you drive a more expensive car than they drive.
Rick Tharp Principal, Tharp Did It

109 Design awards are pure vanity. Except for all the ones we've won.
David Turner Principal, Turner Duckworth

110 If I work on this project any longer I'm going to start ovulating.

Jim Lienhart Principal, Lienhart Design, on an extremely arduous logo design project for a woman's personal hygiene product

111 Often design departments are viewed as little decoration groups. They are viewed as artists who will make stuff look good, not strategic thinkers by any stretch of the imagination. You know, they are just artists. They're clever. They'll make everything look pretty. Well, I can tell you, that doesn't work.
Peter Phillips From *Creating the Perfect Design Brief: Managing Design for Strategic Advantage,* Allworth Press, 2004

112 Being a famous designer is like being a famous dentist.

Noreen Morioka Principal, AdamsMorioka

FREEDOM
"X"

IMAGE WINNING

REVERSE
OR
POS

Vision

113 An ordinary life is a crime.

Eric Schmider Musician

114 I am constantly surprised that it is called "low-brow" art, when it always seems to raise people's eyebrows.

Emek Artist and designer

115 If graphic designers can learn anything from their past, it should be that the best graphic design doesn't use the past to solve the complex problems of the present: it uses the present to reveal the possibilities of the future.

Jeffrey Keedy Designer and CalArts instructor

116 [It brings me] satisfaction to find the remains, almost geologic remains, of a poster that [I] designed, fixed on a street wall, buried behind dozens of overlapped posters.

Alejandro Magallanes Poster designer

117 You have to be careful what you criticize today because it may be a new way of looking at things tomorrow.

Herbert Matter From a clipping the Swiss designer had filed away with his own papers

118 It seems so simple that the design of a place should be focused around an idea and then all disciplines—architecture, interiors, graphics, lighting, even writing—be integrated to communicate that vision. But, take a look around you, and it's obvious that it's obviously not happening enough.

Kiki Obata Principal, Kiku Obata & Company

119 Change for the sake of change has nothing to do with vision.

Jack H. Summerford Designer and writer

120 All projects are different, but you have to treat each one of them with care. Sometimes you get to build a luxury yacht; other times, it'll be a rowboat. You still have to make sure the thing doesn't spring a leak.

Stefan G. Bucher Principal, 344 Design, LLC

KEEP THE FOLLOWING
IN MIND: USUALLY
YOU FEEL BORED, SAD
+ DEPRESSED + LONELY
BEFORE
YOU'VE HAD FOOD OR DONE
YOUR WORK.
LESSON: EAT + WORK

121 We often don't realize that the people we admire as designers have yet to "arrive." Their ongoing quests are part of the reason we admire them so much.

Thomas Vasquez Art director, Cyclops Design

122 Throughout my life, I have been searching for a language that makes it possible to convey to others the world of my inner emotions and pictures which have acquired their own life.

João Machado João Machado Design

123 When I am working on a problem, I never think about beauty. I only think about how to solve the problem. But when I have finished, if the solution is not beautiful, I know it is wrong.

Richard Buckminster Fuller Engineer, theorist, and mathematician

124 [The first graphic designers] did everything from the logo to the actual project, to actually marketing the thing. They did incredible things. That was 75 years ago. I'm just infatuated with those people. If I could go back in time, I would do it.

John Sayles Principal, Sayles Graphic Design

When Peter Vattanathan graduated from Art Center College of Design, his sketchbooks actually ended up being a significant part of his portfolio.

125 It is not the answer that enlightens, but the question.

Eugene Ionesco French playwright

126 Always design a thing by considering it in its next larger context—a chair in a room, a room in a house, a house in an environment, an environment in a city plan.

Eliel Saarinen Furniture designer and architect

127 **Enter your mind, be formless, shapeless, like water. Now you put water into a cup, it becomes a cup; you put water into a bottle, it becomes the bottle; you put it into a teapot, it becomes the teapot. Now water can flow, or it can crash. Be water, my friend.**

Bruce Lee As quoted by Peter Vattanatham

128 Let your hook be always cast; in the pool where you least expect it, there will be a fish.

Ovid Greek philosopher and poet

129 We imagine ourselves able to do anything,
and our software helps us believe that we can...
But we must consider the what and the why.

Neville Brody Designer

130 The good is not a category that interests me.

Rem Koolhaas Architect, principal of OMA, Netherlands

131 # In the name of progress we have sacrificed an inherent need for quietness, for serenity.

Gianni Bortolotti Poster artist

132 Are we uncovering nature or inventing it? Is the "rightness"
that you arrive at in a work an invention or a discovery? Is its appeal a
reflection of the way our brains are wired—to seek and appreciate
sense and pattern—or a deeper insight into the structure of nature itself?

Rian Hughes Device

"I think, therefore I am,"
says Felix Sockwell,
quoting French philosopher
René Descartes.

133 It was never my design objective that the furniture be
different or novel; only that it be good to sit in,
good to use, good to look at, and easy for everyone to buy.

Charles Eames Furniture designer, architect, and filmmaker

134 ## We are what we repeatedly do.

Aristotle Greek philosopoher and mathematician, via Felix Sockwell

135 We help clients see their future.

Ron Miriello Principal, Miriello Grafico

136 [An] aspect which helps me in my creations is
that I find life very interesting, despite its unpredictable
ups and downs. I've grown to enjoy all of the sensations
which are derived from the good times as well as the bad.
[They] not only give me invaluable perceptions of life,
they also give me incredible creative energy.

Kan Tai-Keung Principal, Kan & Lau

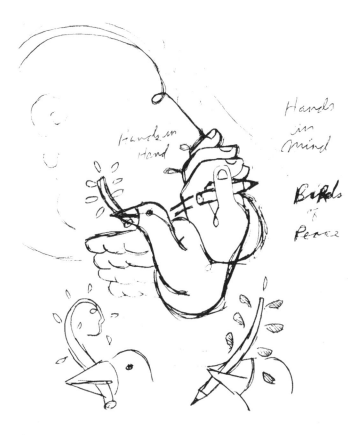

Hands in Hand

Hands in Mind

Birds of Peace

137 A well-defined problem is half solved.

Michael Osborne Principal, Michael Osborne Design

138 Expectations deny discoveries.

Rick Valicenti Thirst

139 The evolution of form begins with the perception of failure.

Henry Petrosk
From *The Evolution of Useful Things*

140 The good is often the enemy of the best.

Voltaire French playwright and philosopher

141 Graphic designers are caught up in a media stream that is very wide and fast, but not very deep. The only way to navigate in it is to go faster or slower than the stream. To go faster, you must be at the forefront of technology and fashion, both of which are changing at an unprecedented rate. To go slower, you need an understanding of context through history and theory. Graphic designers are predisposed to go faster or slower according to their experience and inclination, but mostly they are getting swept along in the currents of pop mediocrity.

Jeffrey Keedy Designer and CalArts instructor

142 I don't believe in art. I believe in artists.

Marcel Duchamp French /US artist and Cubist

143 Whenever I draw a circle, I immediately want to step out of it.

Richard Buckminster Fuller Engineer, theorist, and mathematician

144 However beautiful the strategy, you should occasionally look at the results.

Winston Churchill Prime Minister of England during World War II

145 Accidents often produce the best solutions… only you can recognize the difference between an accident and your original intent.

Jennifer Morla Principal, Morla Design

146 To be great is to be misunderstood; many "artists" simply choose to be misunderstood.

Terry Marks Principal, Terry Marks Design

147 **Creating visual imagery is a state of mind. It involves the reproduction of what we see. But much more than that, it becomes an outlet to express feelings about what we experience.**

Tracy Sabin Principal, Sabingrafik

148 No house should ever be on any hill or on anything. It should be of the hill, belonging to it, so hill and house could live together, each the happier for the other.

Frank Lloyd Wright Architect

149 Doing good design is easy. But doing great design requires a great client.

Michael Osborne Principal, Michael Osborne Design

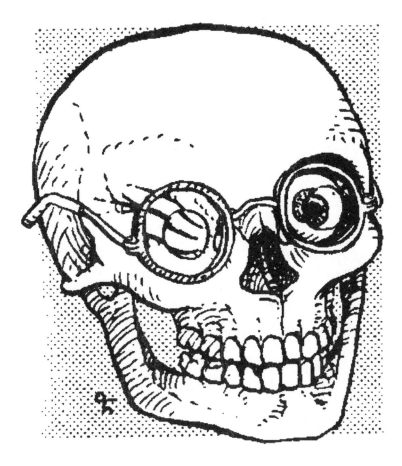

150 A design has no more integrity
than its purpose or subject matter.

Katherine McCoy Design educator

151 Problem solving is not a restrictive art but a liberating one.

Michael Johnson Creative director of Johnson Banks, from his book, *Problem Solved*

152 **An inexperienced observer
sees everything in a picture;
the experienced one sees
even the things that are missing.**

Rastko Ciric Poster designer and instructor,
University of Arts, Belgrade

153 Somewhere there's a handprint in a cave.
Somewhere there's a footprint on a moon.
Somewhere there's an artist with an original idea.

Emek Artist and designer

Do It

154 What I'm trying to produce is the visual equivalent of the chord change that makes the hairs on the back of your neck stand up.

Rian Hughes Principal, Device

155 The most meaningful developments in my work are those that occurred involuntarily and blindly, without my knowing what I was going to do, when I had enough faith in my own creative process to be willing to wait for it to happen without my will demanding it.

Milton Glaser Principal, Milton Glaser Inc., and design educator

156 A legacy is something you build every day.

Jamie Koval Designer at VSA Partners, on the difference between fame and a good reputation, from *Inside the Business of Graphic Design*

157 I've always held to the belief that the practice of creating compelling graphic design occurs not by employing the principles of a democracy, but rather, that of a monarchy.

Thomas Vasquez Art director, Cyclops Design

A visual representation of Alice Drueding's and Joe Scorsone's design relationship, from the artists: "Sketching is one of the languages we use to communicate with one another. It's a form of conversation," says Drueding.

158 At school, no one can teach you how to design a poster, for the poster itself should teach you how to design it.

Alejandro Magallanes Poster designer

159 # Collaborative work is the result of lots of disagreement.

Joe Scorsone and Alice Drueding Designers, principals of Scorsone-Drueding

160 # Good design is not learned— it is realized.

Jesse von Glück Motive Design

161 If we are lucky, we will work many days doing things we are not so thrilled about so we can spend hours doing what we love.

Robert Louey Principal, Louey Rubino Design

162 Good enough
is good enough if
your standards
are high enough.

Steve Frykholm Design director for Herman Miller

163 Beat the dead horse.

Kevin Krueger Designer at
SamataMason, on exploring
ideas to the very ends of
their tails

164 I used to be terrified that I wouldn't do a good enough job.
Now I know that terror and excitement are part of the same
continuum, and I am genuinely excited about my work.

Ethel Kessler Principal, Kessler Design Group

165 The problem with editing is
to choose what should be left in
and what should be left out.

Alejandro Magallanes Poster designer

166 Do what you love and tomorrow will pay the rent.

Felix Sockwell On creating work that will never have a home

167 What moves men of genius, or rather what inspires their work, is not new ideas, but their obsession with the idea that what has already been said is still not enough.

Eugene Delacroix French Romantic painter

168 The next time you see a sixteen-color, blind-embossed, gold-stamped, die-cut, elaborately folded and bound job, printed on handmade paper, see if it isn't a mediocre idea trying to pass for something else.

Milton Glaser Principal, Milton Glaser Inc., and design educator

169 Don't break the rules just to be breaking
the rules, but on the other hand, don't let them
get in the way either.

Rick Tharp Principal, Tharp Did It

170 # Play!

Peter Vattanatham Principal, Lovely Brand

171 Forget all the rules you ever learned about graphic design.
Including the ones in this book.

Bob Gill Founding partner, Pentagram, from the title of his now
renowned book, *Forget All the Rules You Ever Learned About Graphic Design*

172 Do the obvious, then throw it out.

Glenn Mitsui Principal, Glenn Mitsui Design

173 As a young designer, I was often
reminded that there's never growth
without agitation. Thirty years later,
I'm several pounds heavier and still agitated.

Jilly Simon Principal, Concrete

CHICKEN   1 NOT?

- CHICKENS NOT FAT...UP.
-

SIN

Nutrition Facts: Calories 3l.
Fat 14g (22%g (2% DV), Sodiu 6%
rb: 35g (Protein 4g, Vita DV).
C values (DV) are based prie die

AND FRESHNESS
hould reach you in dition. If
0702 M-F, 8:30 astern (Co
ave the unused wrapper

1-5-09

Fiel Valdez of Lovely
Brand says her sketch-
books contain everything:
drawings, writing, lists,
photos, and ephemera
that is stapled, taped,
sewn, or glued onto their
pages, all in "a perfectly
incomprehensible order,"
she adds.

174 Every practice has a set of rules which governs it. Mastery occurs with the realization of these rules. Innovation occurs at the point of intelligent and creative rebellion against them.

Fiel Valdez Principal, Lovely Brand

175 The only true happiness comes from squandering ourselves for a purpose.

John Mason Brown Literary critic

176 Up until the point we commit, we dance about the edges and we deny Providence the ability to add to our own actions. But the moment we do, something happens. People and happenings swing into action on our behalf, simply due to the act of commitment. If there is anything you want to do or dream you can, commit. Commitment has boldness, magic, and power within it. Do it now.

Goethe German playwright and philosopher

Responsibility

177 More than a dozen years ago, I was browsing through a book when I ran across the following unattributed maxim: "The secret of teaching is to appear to have known all your life what you learned this afternoon." I stopped and read this over again. And again. This is not a prescription for teaching, I thought, it's a blueprint for seizing and keeping control. In contrast, the aim of a teacher should be the transfer of power, from teacher to student, and the persuasion of each student to accept responsibility for his or her lifelong education.

Roy R. Behrens Professor of art at the University of Northern Iowa, from *Citizen Designer*

178 Use a unique point of view: your client's.

Earl Gee and Fani Chung Principals, Gee+Chung Design

179 In the matter of layout, forget art at the start and use horse-sense. The printer-designer's whole duty is to make a clear presentation of the message… This calls for an exercise of common sense and faculty of analysis rather than for art.

William Addison Dwiggins Book designer, from *What is Graphic Design?*, published by RotoVision, 2002

180 It's been very important throughout my career that I've met all the guys I've copied, because at each stage they've said, "Don't play like me, play like you."

Eric Clapton Musician

181 The objective in times of [economic] restraint should be to seek excellence, not opulence.
David Craib Principal, Parable Design

182 Companies need an identity, and the logo
is the logical vehicle. But today,
corporations have logos just because
other corporations have logos.
They are terrified of appearing different.
Designers have to be the brave pioneers.
Art Chantry Principal, Art Chantry Design Co.

183 | **Focus on creating client value, not visual.**
Earl Gee and Fani Chung Principals, Gee+Chung Design

184 There are no bad clients, only bad designers.
Bob Gill Founding partner of Pentagram; from *Graphic Design as a Second Language*

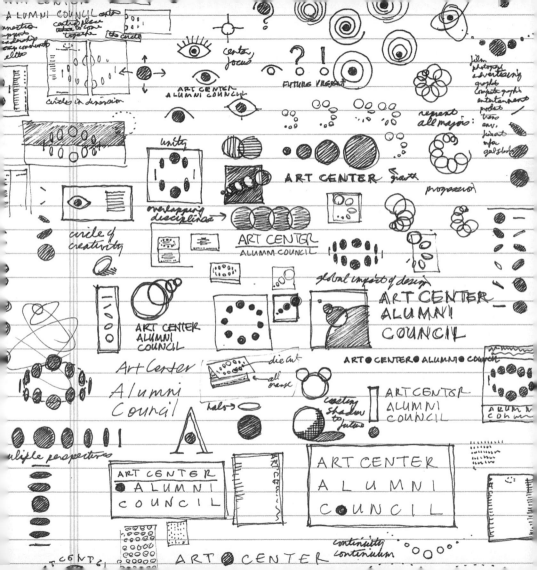

185 If we can produce the kind of art which harnesses the power of the human instinct for the harmony of form, beauty, and cleanness that seems inevitable when you see it… then I think we may be doing a job for clients.

Lester Beall From "The Creative Process of Lester Beall," by R. Roger Remington, *Step-By-Step Graphics*, July/August 1990, pp. 120-129.

186 Whatever the information transmitted, it must, ethically and culturally, reflect its responsibility to society.

Joseph Müller-Brockmann Swiss graphic designer, from *What is Graphic Design?*, RotoVision, 2002

187 For modern advertising and for the modern exponent of form, the individual element—the artist's "own touch"—is of absolutely no consequence.

Lazar Markovitch Lissitzky Russian Constructivist painter and graphic designer

188 For today's youth market, every brand is an accessory and every purchase makes a statement.

Peter van Stolk Founder, Jones Soda Co.

189 To design the future effectively, you must first let go of your past.

Charles J. Givens Financial portfolio designer

190 You must
look
to the past
in order
to see the
future.

Robin Perkins
Principal,
Selbert Perkins
Design

*"All you can eat? Not!"
says Soonduk Krebs, who
created this art.*

191 | Competition is a by-product of productive work, not its goal. A creative man is motivated by the desire to achieve, not by the desire to beat others.

Ayn Rand Russian-born American writer and philosopher who advocated capitalism, individualism, and "objectivism"

192 | A designer… has the true responsibility to give his audiences not what they think they want, for this is almost invariably the usual, the accustomed, the obvious, and hence, the unspontaneous. Rather, he should provide that quality of thought and intuition which rejects the ineffectual commonplace for effectual originality.

Lester Beall From "The Creative Process of Lester Beall," by R. Roger Remington, *Step-By-Step Graphics*, July/August 1990, p. 120-129.

193 | **The moment clients realize that the revisions are not an all-you-can-eat buffet, suddenly, they realize they are not hungry.**

Soonduk Krebs Principal, SK Designworks

194 The most I can do
should be the least
that I attempt.

Tim Hale Fossil

195 I am not so much concerned with the individual
work of art as with the total shape and content of the human scene.

Herbert Bayer German-born American designer (and former
Bauhaus student), 1967

196 Stop looking at yourself as
a designer, and start thinking of
yourself as a deliverer of ideas.

Ståle Melvær Principal, Melvær & Lien, from *Inside the
Business of Graphic Design*

197 I've yet to have a client ask me to make them look smaller than they are.

Bill Gardner Principal, Gardner Design

198 The strategy in communications is not to sell the ¼-inch drill bit,
but the ¼-inch hole. The message needs to be results oriented.

Robert Louey Principal, Louey Rubino Design

199 We need to reposition, to think of design as more than just doing, to allow our work to be the intermediary for being.

Chaz Maviyane-Davies Design consultant and filmmaker

200 Different beats better. Every time.

Greg Galle Designer and member of C2 LLC

201 [The designer holds] a responsibility that embraces the fact that applied good taste is a mark of good citizenship.

Lester Beall Excerpted from *Nine Pioneers in American Graphic Design,* by R. Roger Remington and Barbara J. Hodik

202 The term "client"? I hate it. If I go to see the doctor, technically, I'm his client. I'm paying him, after all. But that doesn't mean I'm in charge. Not if I know what is good for me.

Peter Phillips From *Creating the Perfect Design Brief: Managing Design for Strategic Advantage,* Allworth Press, 2004

203 We live in a society where everybody feels guilty. We want to do good, but we don't want to get out of the house. A brand can help us feel good if you buy this yogurt.

Marc Gobé Author and president, Desgrippes Gobé

204 Other professions, like architecture, to name one, are really sustained and forwarded by criticism. If you open a graphics magazine from the last 30 years, there never seems to be a page of criticism, just attractive biographies and that is it. Do you think we can go on without criticism? Without criticism we will never have a profession.

Massimo Vignelli Speaking at the "Coming of Age" Symposium, Rochester Institute of Technology, 1983

205 We are in the self-expression business. Just not our own.

Greg Galle Designer and member of C2 LLC

206 Graphic designers are, by and large, selfish and spoiled. They stubbornly control and individually design things that are generally smaller than them, perfecting to a level appreciated only by people like them. They don't share and play well with others.

Wayne Hunt Principal, Hunt Design

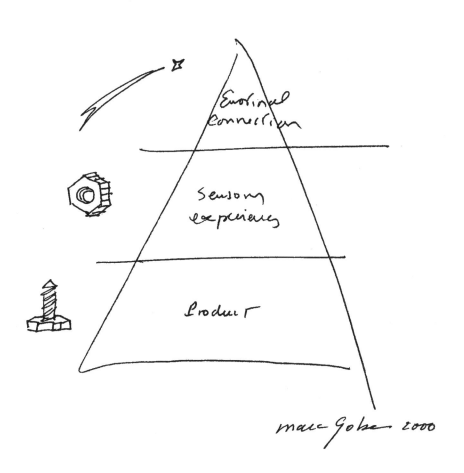

Emotional
Connection

Sensory
experience

Product

marc Gobe 2000

207 High degrees of specialization may be rendering us unable to see the connections between the things we design and their consequences as they ripple out into the biosphere and technosphere in ways we aren't trained to see or may never fully understand.

Terry Irwin Design consultant and educator, from the 2/17/04 issue of *Voice: AIGA Journal of Design*

208 Our best work is the work we do for the sake of others.
It is in the lives and hearts of people we serve that we craft our legacy.

Steffanie Lorig Principal, Lorig Design

209 Practice safe design: Use a concept.

Petrula Vronkitis Principal, Vronkitis Design Office

210 If designers create the trademarks, and advertising agencies do the campaign, who does the bit in between?

Ken Cato Principal, Cato Purnell Partners

211 Many graphic designers do not understand that academia is not just a hothouse of wanton self-expression, but is actually the bastion of tradition. Design practice relies on design education to train people in the latest technology, and to develop basic skills and literacy. But what many designers fail to recognize is that its most important role is in establishing continuity from the past to the future. It is the place where the canon is constantly being elaborated and reformulated. If certain values are deemed important to design, such values will most likely be articulated and perpetuated through education, not practice.

Jeffrey Keedy Designer and CalArts instructor

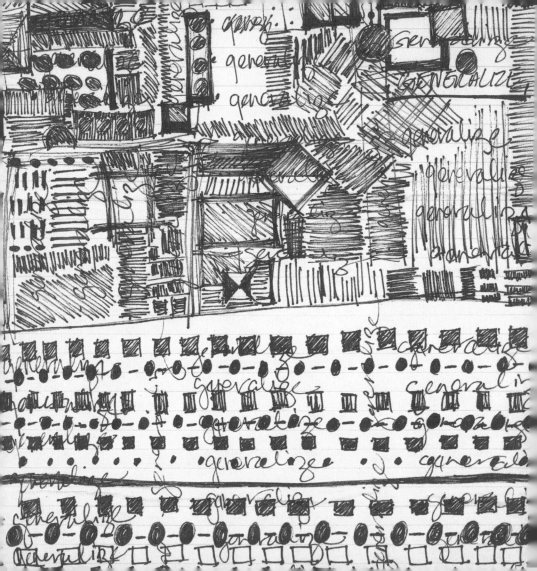

212 A company without design is like a match without flame.

Juan-Carlos Fernández Ideogram, Mexico

213 People tell stories in order to live. Let them.

Sean Adams Principal, Adams Morioka

214 What if we thought of the audience as human beings and not as consumers?

John Creson Art director, Addis

215 Confusion and clutter are failures of design, not attributes of information.

Edward Tufte Designer, artist and author, from *Envisioning Information*

216 Good work begets good work.

Yang Kim Principal, BBK

217 Business wants [the designer] to help create an attitude about the facts, not to communicate them. And only about some of the facts.

William Golden Longtime art director at CBS

Tools

218 I became a graphic artist because of the tools. I love working at a big drawing table with traditional tools: T-squares, compasses, mechanical pencils, French curves, black ink, and graphite. At a computer, one works on a keyboard. I never considered myself a typist.

Michael Schwab Principal, Michael Schwab Studio

219 Although I admit the computer has made my job as a designer much easier in many ways, it has also made the process a lot less pleasant.

Rick Tharp Principal, Tharp Did It

220 Is it a vehicle or a weapon? Wit needs no reason.

Seymour Chwast Founding partner of Push Pin Studios, from *The Left-Handed Designer*

221 Archives can be treasure troves in sensitive hands or theme parks if over-exploited. [It is] a case of knowing what to leave out, or in, and [when] to step back before going forward.

Mary Lewis Principal, Lewis Moberly

222 The poster starts where words end.

Péter Pócs Hungarian poster designer

223 The defining qualities of contemporary information culture are power and play, because never before have we been able to change the conditions of experimentation so easily and dynamically... Consider the designer who changes the background color again and again in hopes of pleasing the client... She is engaged in "tweaking" the system, using its power to play with the variables in real time.

Peter Lunenfeld Art Center College of Design

224 When Einstein realized, "Dear me, this universe with its wonders all adds up to $E=mc^2$?," he did not stop to think whether this concept would sell better set in Futura or Antikva.

Kari Piippo Graphic designer, on how fundamental truths are not affected by design

225 A personal style is like a handwriting—it happens as the byproduct of our way of seeing things, enriched by the experiences of everything around us.

Massimo Vignelli Designer, from *Becoming a Graphic Designer*

226 The only place Avant Garde
looks good is in the words "Avant Garde."

Tony DeSpigna Partner of Herb Lubalin,
who designed the typeface

227 A trademark is created by
a designer, but made by a corporation.

Paul Rand Designer and art director

228 A ubiquitous and successful corporate identity is, in the last resort,
a calamity just because it is ubiquitous.

Ken Garland Designer and art director

229 Having a flag that has change built into it—
as every time you change a state or you add a
state, you change a star. That makes an
ever-changing symbol of, to me, a somewhat
ever-changing country. From a graphic designer's
point of view, where we're always involved in
creating these relatively tight guidelines…
to have something as loose as this and still have
it retain its symbolic power is pretty magical.

Kit Hinrichs Designer and American flag collector, from a "Studio 360" broadcast

230 When we feel less secure,
with less control over our daily lives,
we reach out to brands to
connect with a time when things
seemed better.

Marc Gobé Author and president, Desgrippes Gobé

231 Most trademarks don't look that good on the radio.

Ken Cato Principal, Cato Purnell Partners

232 With 26 soldiers of lead I have conquered the world.

Francis Meynell Printer-typographer, from the title of an article he
wrote in 1923, reproduced in *What is Graphic Design?*, Rotovision, 2002

233 To be truly useful, any technology has to be unconscious…
We don't pick up a hammer to have a "hammer-and-nail experience."

Bill Viola Video artist

234 I say this to myself every day, or maybe I hear it in my head: "God lives in the details."

Matt Collins Zipatoni

235 Typography bears much resemblance to cinema, just as the reading of print puts the reader in the role of movie projector. The reader moves the series of imprinted letters before him with a speed consistent with apprehending the motions of the author's mind.

László Moholoy-Nagy Hungarian-born artist and Bauhaus instructor, 1925

236 When in Rome, use Times Roman.

Marty Neumeier
Neutron LLC

237 Typography is the particle physics of design.

Rian Hughes Device

239 Typography is what
language looks like.
Ellen Lupton Director of the
MFA program at the
Maryland Institute College of Art

238 The more
uninteresting
a letter, the
more useful it
is to the
typographer.

Piet Zwart
Dutch typographer,
photographer, and
industrial designer

240 I heard Herb Lubalin say Helvetica was the most
destructive face that was ever invented; it was just the
total downfall of good typography… because you
can't make any mistakes. It just kind of numbs you
out. It's so perfect, it's dead, stillborn.
Rudy VanderLans Founder of Émigré, from *PRINT* magazine, September/October 1992

241 Helvetica. To look further is vain.
Massimo Vignelli Principal, Vignelli Associates, circa 1970

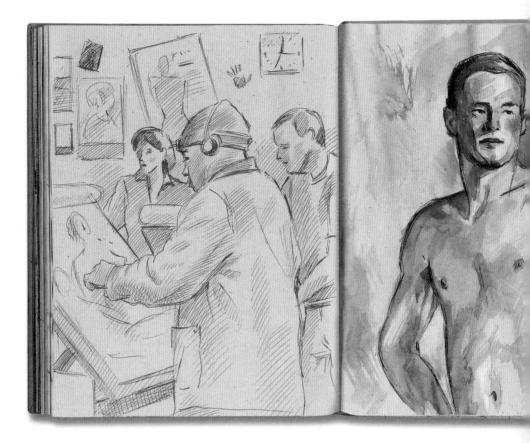

Tracy Sabin has attended an open sketching session, sponsored by the San Diego Society of Illustrator's chapter, for 20 years. Sometimes he sketches the model, and sometimes he sketches the class itself.

242 Brands do not conquer markets. They don't have armies. They are citizens of the world.

Marc Gobé Author and president, Desgrippes Gobé

243 Be niggardly with decorations, borders, and such accessories. Do not pile up ornaments like flowers at a funeral. Get acquainted with the shapes of the type letters themselves. Pick good ones and stick with them.

William Addison Dwiggins Book designer

244 **Over the years, a collection of sketchbooks becomes a kind of diary of people and events and of your development as an artist.**

Tracy Sabin Principal, Sabingrafik

245 Without contrast, you're dead.

Paul Rand Designer and art director

246 The best design tool is a long eraser with a pencil at one end.

Marty Neumeier Neutron LLC

247 Imagine that you have before you a flagon of wine. You may choose your own favorite vintage for this imaginary demonstration, so that it be a deep shimmering crimson in color. You have two goblets before you. One is of solid gold, wrought in the most exquisite patterns. The other is of crystal-clear glass, thin as a bubble, and as transparent. Pour and drink; and according to your choice of goblet, I shall know whether or not you are a connoisseur of wine. For if you have no feelings about wine one way or the other, you will want the sensation of drinking the stuff out of a vessel that may have cost thousands of pounds; but if you are a member of that vanishing tribe, the amateurs of fine vintages, you will choose the crystal, because everything about it is calculated to reveal rather than to hide the beautiful thing which it was meant to contain.

Beatrice Ward From *The Crystal Goblet—Sixteen Essays on Typography*, 1956, on what typography should do

248 It is [Beatrice Ward's] greatest failing as a type critic that she never mentioned (or, apparently, even considered) the jelly jar. Drinking wine from a jelly jar reveals the color of the wine and saves both money and landfill space.

Gunnar Swanson From "Serif: On the Democratization of Typography," Fall 1996 issue of the *AIGA Journal of Graphic Design*

249 How can there be too many
typefaces in the world?
Are there too many songs,
too many books, too many
places to go?

Rian Hughes Device

250 Matthew Carter's Bell Centennial font
was designed for maximum legibility
at a minimum size. It is used in the US
phone books. Bell Centennial has saved
millions of trees.

Ellen Lupton Director of the MFA program at
the Maryland Institute College of Art

251 The best designers can make music on any instrument.

Anne Traver Principal, Methodologie

252 Graphic design's process is similar to haute cuisine. We have a
guest ready to be delighted. We have our own space, the tools, and
a team. But inevitably, we have to go out to the market and search
for the right ingredients to get inspired.

Julio Ferro FutureBrand Argentina

253 A symbol is language at the
molecular level.

Marty Neumeier Neutron LLC

Creativity

254 If you have a great idea, it will tell you how to execute it.

Jack H. Summerford Designer and writer

255 Art cannot be taught. Artists are born that way. They educate themselves, or else they do not become educated.

James Montgomery Flagg From "Celebrity Virtuoso: James Montgomery Flagg," by Frederic B. Taraba, *Step-By-Step Graphics,* November/December 1989, pp. 116–123.

256 A lady sitting next to Raymond Loewy at dinner struck up a conversation.

"Why," she asked, "did you put two Xs in Exxon?"

"Why ask?" he asked.

"Because," she said, "I couldn't help noticing."

"Well," he responded, "that's the answer."

Unknown From *The Art of Looking Sideways,* by Alan Fletcher

257 A good concept is the fruit of an analytical, as well as intuitive, process.

Fang Chen Poster artist and instructor

258 Creativity can solve almost any problem. The creative act, the defeat of habit by originality, overcomes everything.

George Lois Designer and Madison Avenue icon

Raphael Henry is a Swiss architect and designer who develops brands and brand environments. He works frequently with Fossil.

259 Our job is in the delineation of the problem, not necessarily in providing creative.

Michael Vanderbyl Principal, Vanderbyl Design; on working with identity projects, from the LogoLounge.com website

260 A creative solution always lies at the fingertips holding the drawing pencil.

Raphael Henry From his website, thebrandstorm.com

261 I generally think that the idea is the starting point of graphic design. The second step is to find the appropriate style to make this idea work the best.

Christoph Niemann Designer and illustrator, *Novum Online,* August 2002

262 **The same hand can draw art for the sake of emotional expression and design that serves a purpose.**

Raphael Henry From his website thebrandstorm.com

263 Inspiration is intention obeyed.

Emily Carr Artist and author

264 A hunch is creativity trying to tell you something.

Frank Capra Filmmaker

265 Creativity often consists of merely turning up what is already there. Did you know that right and left shoes were thought up only a little more than a century ago?

Bernice Fitz-Gibbon Retail advertising pioneer

266 The source of the creative impulse is a mystery... Ideas may come from anywhere, anything, any time, any place... They spring from rather unromantic, sometimes unexpected, or even unsavory sources.

Paul Rand Designer and art director

267 Every creative act
is a sudden cessation
of stupidity.

Edward Herbert Land
Designer of the Polaroid camera

268 Creativity requires a sandbox
larger than ink on paper.

Clement Mok Designer

269 Creativity consists of coming up with many ideas, not just that one great idea.

Charles Thompson Filmmaker

270 My curiosity is my creativity on the way to discovery.

Unknown

271 The creative person wants to be a know-it-all. He wants
to know about all kinds of things: ancient history,
nineteenth-century mathematics, current manufacturing
techniques, flower arranging, and hog futures. Because
he never knows when these ideas might come together
to form a new idea. It may happen six minutes later,
or six months, or six years down the road. But he has faith
that it will happen.

Carl Ally Principal, Ally & Gargano; advertiser and
self-described "grenade thrower"

Scenes from an Italian restaurant—really—made with chalk, house paint, and collaged found visuals by Ron Miriello, during his frequent visits to Italy.

272 | We're all naturally curious when we're eight years old. But as most people get older, they become less and less curious, so they ask other people to be curious for them. That's what I do for a living.

Ron Miriello Principal, Miriello Grafico

273 | To live a creative life, we must lose our fear of being wrong.

Joseph Chilton Pearce Writer and philosopher

274 | Creativity is essentially a lonely art. An even lonelier struggle. To some a blessing. To others a curse. It is in reality the ability to reach inside yourself and drag forth from your very soul an idea.

Lou Dorfsman Legendary art director at CBS

275 | Observation is more searching when it is acting for the memory than when used for immediate transcription.

John Gannam Illustrator, from *Forty Illustrators and How They Work*

Wayne Hunt of Hunt Design carries a sketch-book everywhere— on business trips, into the front yard, through airports, to concerts. There's nothing that a Uni-Ball pen can't capture, he says.

276 I am a happy invalid, and it has revolutionized my whole attack. I will produce art on paper and wood after my own heart with no heed to any market.

William Addison Dwiggins Book designer, after being diagnosed with diabetes in 1922 and vowing to refuse all future commercial work

277 Creative thinking is no substitute for hard work.

Unknown

278 Creativity is allowing yourself to make mistakes. Art is knowing which ones to keep.

Scott Raymond Adams American cartoonist and creator of Dilbert

279 [Sketching] is not really about the finished drawing, which is usually no great thing anyway. It's about looking and drawing as a simultaneous activity. It's really about the art of being there.

Wayne Hunt Principal, Hunt Design

280 | **No one ever discovered anything new by coloring inside the lines.**

Thomas Vasquez Art director, Cyclops Design

281 So-called concepts are nothing but mental reassurances for designers themselves, to create risklessly, without creating the new.

Jan Wilker Principal, Karlssonwilker, Inc.

282 I try not to think out of the box anymore, but on its edge, its corner, its flap, and under its bar code.

Clint Runge Archrival

283 Designers will no longer be paid for graphics—only for ideas.

Ken Cato Principal, Cato Purnell Partners

284 Imagination is what distinguishes an artist from a mechanic.

John Gannam Illustrator, from *Forty Illustrators and How They Work*

285 [Creativity is] to create with open perception.
Stefan Sagmeister Principal, Sagmeister, Inc.

286 Art is a long dream under a short deadline.
Emek Artist and designer

287 Limited means beget new forms, invite creation,
make the style. Progress in art does not lie in extending
its limits, but in knowing them better.
Georges Braque Cubist painter; from *A Designer's Art,* by Paul Rand

288 As the speed of change accelerates,
the value of newness diminishes.
Karrie Jacobs Design critic and journalist

289 Images transport ideas, but design drives them.
Chaz Maviyane-Davies Design consultant and filmmaker

290 For me, insanity is super sanity. The normal is psychotic. Normal means lack of imagination, lack of creativity.

Jean Dubuffet French painter and sculptor

291 Less is only more where more is no good.

Frank Lloyd Wright Architect

292 Don't try to be original, just try to be good. If you're original, then you're original.

Paul Rand Designer and art director

This is a page from Steffanie Lorig's sketchbook. The designer is director of Art With Heart, a Seattle outreach program that brings designers and their skills together with ill and/or homeless youth to help them through critical periods in their lives.

293 Create, artist! Do not talk!

Johann Wolfgang von Goethe German playwright and philosopher

294 On the smallest level, creativity can alter moods. On the grandest level, it can change lives.

Steffanie Lorig Principal, Lorig Design

295 Creativity provides opportunity; innovation provides leadership.

Tim Hale Fossil

For the heart that's free
life is a celebration of beauty
a festival of the Spirit

CONSERVAZIONE DEGLI ANTICHI CATASTI

PROVINCIA _Firenze_

UFFICIO _di_ ....

N. d'ordine della domanda (2) ....

PROVINCIA _Firenze_

UFFICIO DISTRETTUALE DELLE IMPOSTE

_di_ .... _Anno 194 3_

N. d'ord. .... (2)

Anno 193 ....

DOMANDA DI VOLTURA che viene presentata a termine dell'art. 6 del R. decreto ......
24 marzo 190 ...., n. 21°, per i pagamenti aggi di proprietà o di possesso dipendenti: ....

Il Richiedente

COPIE OD ESTRATTI DI DOCUMENTI UNITI ALLA DOMANDA

Numero pro-gressivo	SPECIE		SPECIE

Ron Miriello bought a stack of turn-of-the-century house deeds at a thrift shop in Italy and frequently sketches, paints, and draws right on top of them. This one is in colored pencil on a deed from Vinci—home of Leonardo—and shows the top of St. Marks in Venice.

296 If I create from the heart, nearly everything works; if from the head, almost nothing.

Marc Chagall French painter

297 Creativity is in everyone; it just manifests itself differently with each person. My CPA, for example, is one of the most creative people I know. He's a true left-brain, right-brain blended thinker, but he'd never consider himself creative. The form his efforts take just don't register with anyone as creativity. Amazingly creative things happen around us every day and escape in forms we don't recognize.

Ron Miriello Principal, Miriello Grafico

298 Inspiration is hogwash. My work comes directly out of my loves and hates. Muses don't whisper in my ear, and ideas don't flow over my body like a cool rain. I work hard. I always have. And I try to be honest.

James Victore Designer, from the book, *Inspiration = Ideas*, by Petrula Vronkitis

Advice

299 Don't mistake legibility for communication.

David Carson Principal, David Carson Design

300 Be gracious with yourself.

Terry Marks Principal, Terry Marks Design

301 Making good design is easy. It's polishing the half-assed stuff that takes time.

Stefan G. Bucher Principal, 344 Design, LLC

302 The basic premise of

my work is this:

The message must be

succinct, immediate,

and legible from way

across the room.

Michael Schwab
Principal, Michael Schwab Studio

303 Leave the back door unlocked.

Laurie Haycock Makela Cranbrook Academy of Art

304 Every child is an artist. The problem is how to remain an artist once he grows up.
Pablo Picasso Spanish-born painter and co-founder of Cubism

305 Talk to people other than designers.
Simon Dixon and Aporva Baxi Principals, Dixon Baxi

306 The only way to succeed is to learn how to fail—and to have love for those failings.
John Fante Author and playwright

307 To construct, start with deconstruction.
Rina De Maggio RDYA Argentina (RDYA/Drab and Associates Design Group)

308 Focus or fail. You cannot serve multiple masters.
Michelle Fiocca Principal, FocusBalanceCreate

309 To design the future effectively, you must first let go of your past.
Charles J. Givens Financial portfolio designer

310 Don't believe your own hype.

Simon Dixon and Aporva Baxi Principals, Dixon Baxi

311 Use for drying hair and not the other purpose.

Sticker on a hand-held hair dryer in a Japanese hotel bathroom,
spotted by **Robin Perkins and Clifford Selbert,** Selbert Perkins Design

312 Whether you think you can or whether you think you can't—you are right.

Henry Ford Founder, Ford Motor Company

313 Creative energy is a constant presence in our lives, but more often
than not it gets drowned out by the urgency of day-to-day activity.
Designers need to create a space for themselves that is free of interference,
a space that allows them to hear their own intuition.

Petrula Vrontikis Principal, Vronkitis Design Office

314 The wisest men follow their own direction.

Euripides, Greek playwright

315 # Fail fast.

John Creson Addis

316 You know you've achieved perfection in design, not when you have nothing more to add, but when you have nothing more to take away.

Antoine de Saint-Exupéry French pilot, writer, and poet

317 ## Paint a little less of the facts and a little more of the spirit.

Harvey Dunn From "Harvey Dunn: The Gift of Inspiration," by Charles J. Andres, *Step-By-Step Graphics*, March/April 1989, pp. 128-134.

318 # Begin with the end in mind.

Lana Rigsby Principal, Rigsby Design

319 Color theory for life: Those who spend their lives only chasing green end up blue.

Tim Hale Fossil

"Instead of thinking from point A to point B, go from A to M," advises designer John Bielenberg.

320 # Thinking wrong can be right.

John Bielenberg Principal, C2 LLC

321 Listen to your client, take into consideration all of their input, weigh the options, study the details, know the target audience, and then, if necessary, ignore all of it and design what you think will work best.

Von R. Glitschka Principal, Glitschka Studios

322 "Less is more" is [our] principle— everything must earn its space.

Mary Lewis Principal, Lewis Moberly

323 If you dig a hole and it's in the wrong place, digging it deeper isn't going to help.

Seymour Chwast Founding partner of Push Pin Studios, from *The Left-Handed Designer*

324 Look for people to communicate with, not [just for] admirers.

Chaz Maviyane-Davies Design consultant and filmmaker

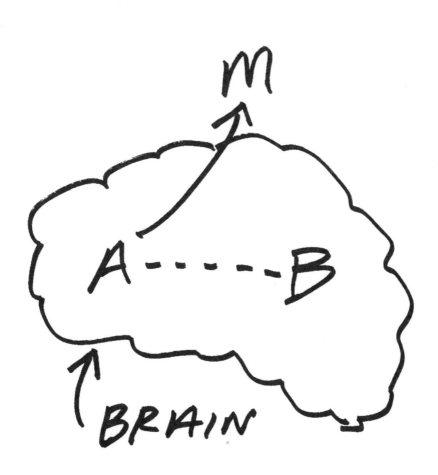

325 Solving the problem is more important than being right.

Milton Glaser Principal, Milton Glaser Inc. and design educator

326 The space in between is as important as the space occupied.

Jennifer Morla Principal, Morla Design

327 A foolish consistency is the hemoglobin of an identity.

Gunnar Swanson Principal, Gunnar Swanson Design Office, with help from Ralph Waldo Emerson

328 Communication that doesn't take a chance, doesn't stand a chance.

Carlos Segura Principal, Segura Inc.

329 Good looks attract people, but personality keeps them interested.

David Turner Principal, Turner Duckworth

330 Choose balance over symmetry.
Anyone can center anything.

Thomas Vasquez Art director, Cyclops Design

331 I'm just now beginning to understand how much is on the shoulders of an editor. It's made me realize what an insignificant part of the project design is. Of course, it's important, but not as important as designers think it is. Designers should get a life, get out there and see the other aspects of the project. If the bones don't work, you've got a pile of skin.

Samuel Antupit Longtime art director on book design, from *365: AIGA Year in Design 22*

332 Minds are like parachutes. They only function when they are open.

Sir James Dewar Inventor of the vacuum flask, better known as the Thermos

333 Be stimulated by rejection.

Bob Gill Founding partner, Pentagram

334 Remember Lot's wife: Avoid the backward glance.

Sean Adams Principal, Adams Morioka

335 Packaging is no good if the box is empty.

Mirko Ilić Principal, Mirko Ilić Corp.

336 Everything you need to know is already in your head. You just have to find it.

Garth Walker Principal, Orange Juice Design

337 No ITC fonts. Ever.

Steve Liska Principal, Liska & Associates

338 Life is not a job.

Michelle Fiocca Principal, FocusBalanceCreate, on separating life from work

339 Art directors should spend more time thinking and less time polishing the firewood.

Carl Warner *Communication Arts,* DDB Needham

LIFE IS NOT A JOB

An ironical page from
a sketchbook that
David Turner has used
in a branding class
that he teaches.

340 It is a lot easier to be new than it is to be good. The criteria for being new is only based on the past few years, but the criteria for being good is based on everything we have learned since the beginning of time.

Jeffrey Keedy Designer and CalArts instructor

341 **A pack[age] should have looks, brains, and personality: to attract, convince, and start a relationship.**

David Turner Principal, Turner Duckworth

342 If you want to win an award, make it bigger. And red.

Steve Liska Principal, Liska & Associates

343 The pushy bird gets the worm.

Sean Adams Principal, Adams Morioka

344 You'll never realize how much you didn't learn in school until you try to teach in one.

Chris Pullman VP, Branding and Visual Communications, WGBH, Boston

Tips for Success

Get ahead of yourself

Steal stuff

Use clichés

Ask

Keep it ruthlessly single mind-
ed.

Kim Baer, in searching
for visual solutions, often
finds herself sketching
a Venn diagram.
"It's something of an
archetypal symbol for
me," she says. "It seems
it's so often where two
apparently divergent
or opposite thoughts
intersect that something
new is revealed."

345 When I was moving to Hong Kong and was about to make a lot of money,
Tibor Kalman told me, "Don't you go and spend the money they pay you, or
you're going to be the whore of the ad agencies for the rest of your life."
I didn't and got easily out again. Most of my colleagues did not get that great
advice and are still stuck in agencies.

Stefan Sagmeister Principal, Sagmeister, Inc.

346 Think 8 hours, work 2 hours.

Mirko Ilić Principal, Mirko Ilić Corp.

347 **So much of my life as a designer is spent
carefully listening to hours of conversations and
scanning reams of documents—sifting for clues,
watching for patterns, looking for the glint of
something possible that's hidden in the mix.**

Kim Baer Principal, KBDA

348 I try to be as stupid as possible regarding my profession,
which means I try to look at as few design magazines as possible.

Ettore Sottsass Principal, Sottsass Associati, from *Wired* magazine, Issue 9.01, January 2001

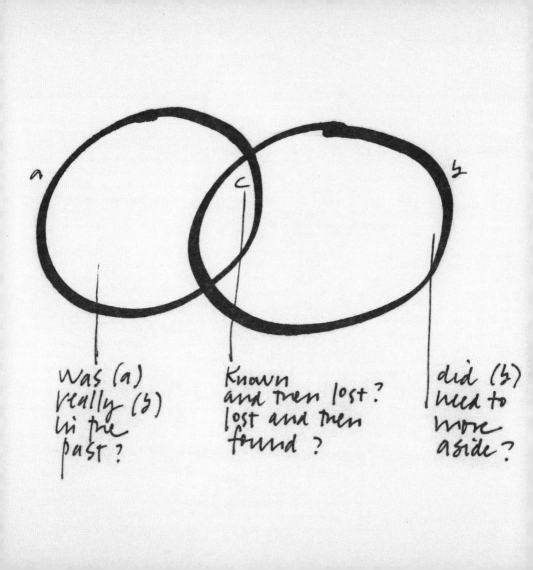

a

c

b

Was (a)
really (b)
in the
past?

Known
and then lost?
lost and then
found?

did (b)
need to
move
aside?

San Francisco illustrator
Ward Shumaker heard
designer Rick Tharp say,
during a lecture, that
when he runs out of
ideas, he goes Dumpster-
diving behind the studios
of famous designers.

349 Part of giving good service is knowing when not to provide any.
Stefan G. Bucher Principal, 344 Design

350 # If you don't risk it, no biscuit.
Sean Adams Principal, Adams Morioka

351 If you have arrived, you had better hang it up and go away.
There is no more reason to continue. We never arrive.
Terry Marks Principal, Terry Marks Design

352 **When you get stuck for an idea, go out and
rummage through the Dumpsters behind
famous designers' studios. There's a wealth
of visual stimuli in there.**

Rick Tharp Principal, Tharp Did It

353 Does it solve the problem? Is it serviceable? How is it going to look in ten years?
Charles Eames Furniture designer, architect, and filmmaker

Reality Check

354 For [the client], it's like naming a baby. You might be talking with very intelligent people about strategy and positioning, but once you present the design, they forget all about that: they immediately start talking about what they like.

Bill Chiaravelle Office of Bill Chiaravelle, on working with clients on logo design projects

355 Any system that sees aesthetics as irrelevant, that separates the artist from the product, that fragments the work of the individual, or creates by committee, or makes mincemeat of the creative process will in the long run diminish not only the product but the maker as well.

Paul Rand Designer and art director, from his book, *A Designer's Art*

356 For every 100 of you, one of you will make it. The rest of you are just fodder for that one.

Laura Zeck *Short Stories*, quoting an art school professor who told this to his class

357 The search for the Holy Grail is not about finding it, but being worthy enough to seek it out.

Robert Louey Principal, Louey Rubino Design

358 We always have to remind clients that a logo is a symbol of what they do: It is not the company or the brand. It is not an identity.

Jack Anderson Principal, Hornall Anderson Design Works, from the LogoLounge.com website

359 # Sometimes we are more fascinated by the forms than by the substance.

Alejandro Magallanes Poster designer

360 An old surrealist trick was to take images that had no business being together and plopping them into the same image. Your mind wants to make associations. Design does that all the time. Punk graphics have always used that. Get [a picture of] a screaming baby and put it next to "Butthole Surfers," and people are horrified. And it's totally innocent! It's just ink on paper, for Christ's sake.

Art Chantry Principal, Art Chantry Design Co.

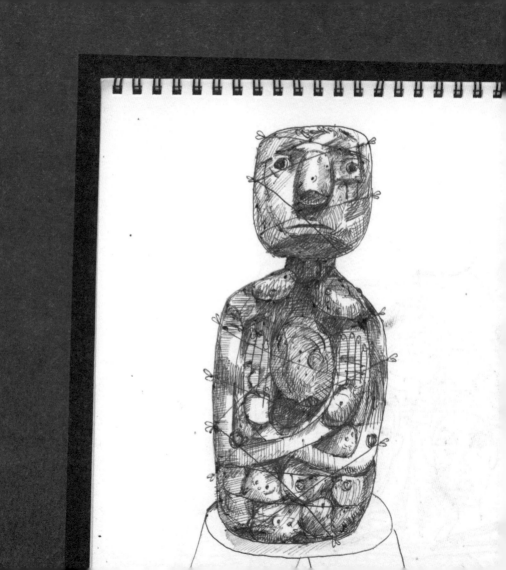

361 Style=fart

Stefan Sagmeister
Principal, Sagmeister Design

362 It's not the paper's fault that so much shit is printed.

Alejandro Magallanes Poster designer

363 Once design didn't have much conscious history. You just did it.
Now that we have a history and people are actually writing about it,
ironically, few young people know anything about it.

Chris Pullman VP, Branding and Visual Communications, WGBH, Boston

364 Boards don't hit back.

Bruce Lee Via Glenn Mitsui, Glenn Mitsui Design

365 I never intended to run a company.
I just wanted to do great design.

Margo Chase Principal, Margo Chase Design, from
Inside the Business of Graphic Design

366 We can't just design an item that looks great. We also have to anticipate how it is boxed up, distributed, and shipped, as well as whether or not a seventeen-year-old kid with a summer job can stock it on the store shelf without ruining it.

Robin Perkins Principal, Selbert Perkins Design

367 If you call it an idea, it's verbal, not visual.

Ralph Schraivogel Swiss poster designer, from "The Flat Earth," by Dan Nadel, *PRINT* magazine, May/June 2004

368 All profoundly original art looks ugly at first.

Clement Greenberg Art critic

369 Like style merchants, [some graphic designers] pick and choose from what is currently hip and readily acceptable to infuse the work of their clients with a dose of contemporary cool.

Rudy VanderLans Writing in *Émigré #64*

370 | **India is vibrant, definitive, over the top, and a visual feast. [Indian] designers and clients should stop looking westward and concentrate on what's outside their window.**

Rabia Gupta RGD

371 | It's not a problem of being a woman in a man's world. It's being a type designer in a world that gives little recognition to this art form.

Zuzana Licko Type designer for *Émigré,* in *Eye* magazine, 2002

372 | There is no recipe for a good layout. What must be maintained is a feeling of change and contrast. A layout man should be simple with good photographs. He should perform acrobatics when the pictures are bad.

Alexy Brodovitch From the *Communication Arts* website

373 | A lot of people in this business develop huge egos. Why? None of us is curing cancer. None of us is saving babies from burning buildings. We're just a bunch of overpaid knuckleheads who think up nutty stuff for some other knuckleheads' products.

Paul Howalt Principal, Howalt Design Studio

374 You may go out for a beer with your clients, you may give them discounts, you may help them with their internal presentations, you may send them nice Christmas cards, and win tons of awards. But they pay you for the work you do.

Christoph Rohrer KMS Team, from *Inside the Business of Graphic Design*, Allworth Press, 2003

375 There is nothing glamorous about what I do. I am a working man.

Saul Bass From the *Communication Arts* website

376 A confident client will see your confidence as strength, not arrogance.

Diti Katona Principal, Concrete, from *Inside the Business of Graphic Design*, Allworth Press, 2003

377 [I believe] there are certain things in life that should be able to be done with a handshake, or else all of the joy is legislated out of life.

Sheree Clark Designer, Sayles Graphic Design, from *Inside the Business of Graphic Design*, Allworth Press, 2003

378 Quotes are kind of scary. You never know when you're going to contradict yourself or back into a lie.

Eric Baldwin Butler, Shine, Stern & Partners

379 We unfortunately live in a corporate world where group decision making is made to avoid failure rather than to achieve success.

Bill Cahan Principal, Cahan & Associates, in a talk to the Association of Registered Graphic Designers of Ontario

380 At one point, if you have a job, no matter who you are, your work will be taken away from you. I don't think that you can adjust your sensibilities beyond a certain point. You can make some accommodations, but the people who are endlessly adaptable are hacks. If you can last 30 or 40 years and still have your work looking fresh, well, you're doing very well.

Milton Glaser Principal, Milton Glaser, Inc., and design educator

381 You can't define exactly, or how, the viewer will take in your visual message. There is an endless number of possible ways of looking at it. The only thing I can do as a designer is to animate the person through my message. He himself should act, should analyze, and reproduce the visual message for himself.

Richard Feurer Studio Eclat, from *PRINT*, November/December 1990

382 I don't think that
design needs theory,
but I think
designers need theory.

Johanna Drucker
Designer and theorist

383 Designers
tend to whisper,
ad agencies
tend to shout.

David Stuart The Partners

384 The word "new," when applied to graphic design,
does not mean "never before."

Steven Heller *New York Times Book Review* art director, and **Mirko Ilić,**
principal of Mirko Ilić Corp., from their book, *Genius Moves*

385 Letters are things, not pictures of things.

Eric Gill Type designer and essayist

386 Although the majority call themselves designers,
there really are two very separate groups: production artists
and designers. Production artists are computer geeks
dressed in black, and designers are artists dressed in black.

Anonymous

387 The best work comes from an art director who allows the team to extend an idea by pushing the boundaries, and who is willing to credit the team on a job well done.

Peter Watts Principal, Watts Design, from *Inside the Business of Graphic Design*, Allworth Press, 2003

388 In all affairs it's a healthy thing now and then to hang a question mark on the things you have long taken for granted.

Bertrand Russell Mathematician and philosopher

389 The way something looks is the last thing we figure out.

Alexander Isley Principal, Alexander Isley Design

390 Even if it is true that commonplace advertising and exhibitions of bad taste are indicative of the mental capacity of the man in the street, the opposing argument is equally valid. Bromidic advertising catering to that bad taste merely perpetuates that mediocrity and denies him one of the most easily accessible means of aesthetic development.

Paul Rand Designer and art director, from his *Thoughts on Design* series

391 For graphic design to be great it needs to be profoundly about you. And the most important thing to remember is that it has nothing to do with you.

Gunnar Swanson Principal, Gunnar Swanson Design Office

Kevin Budelmann's sketches are not necessarily explorations of assigned jobs. Instead, they free his mind to wander outside of normal day-to-day business.

392 I look for three things in a project: 1) Compelling work; 2) fun client; 3) astronomical fees. However, to have a successful project, I really only need two out of the three. For example, I'll do great work with fun people for nothing and still feel rewarded. Or, I'll do great work for a mean, stupid client for outrageous money. Or, I'll do boring work with somebody I like a lot for more money than one can imagine. Anytime I am faced with only one of the three, it is time to rethink the relationship. Actually, it is time to move on.
Lowell Williams Pentagram

393 Only work with people you'd invite to your home for a meal.
Garth Walker Principal, Orange Juice Design

394 # We value what we understand.
Kevin Budelmann Principal, BBK

395 The truly talented people are also the nicest, because they know how hard this all is.
Garth Walker Principal, Orange Juice Design

396 Understanding stops action.
Friedrich Nietzsche German philosopher, from his book *The Will to Power*

397 | **Once we thought design was about balance;
now we look forward to falling off.**
Ingred Sidie and Michelle Sonderegger Principals, Design Ranch

398 Some people are toxic. Avoid them.
Milton Glaser Principal, Milton Glaser Inc., and design educator

399 Once, what you were making was an object; now, it is more often an experience.
Chris Pullman VP, Branding and Visual Communications, WGBH, Boston

400 Graphic designers… find themselves in the role of visual
dishwashers for the Information Architects' chefs.
Gunnar Swanson Principal, Gunnar Swanson Design Office

401 The difference between regulated architects and unregulated
designers is, unlike buildings, letterheads don't fall down and kill people.
Brian Webb Principal, Webb & Webb; formerly Trickett & Webb

Index of Contributors

About the Author

Catharine Fishel specializes in working with and writing about designers and related industries. Her writing has appeared in many leading publications, including *PRINT, Communication Arts, Graphis ID*, and many others. She is editor of the website LogoLounge.com and is the author of many books about design, including *Paper Graphics, Minimal Graphics, Redesigning Identity, The Perfect Package, Designing for Children, LogoLounge, LogoLounge II, Inside the Business of Graphic Design*, and *How to Grow as a Graphic Designer*.

Acknowledgments

Many thanks to Kristin Ellison, who gave me the opportunity to learn so much; for Petrula Vronkitis, who gave me the encouragement to pursue the project; and to all of the contributors to this book, who are a constant source of wisdom and inspiration.